Intermediate
〈中級〉

Ultimate Listening
無敵リスニング

英語力を伸ばす
ディクトグロスタスク30

30 Dictogloss activities to improve
your English skills

Adrian Leis・Simon Cooke

開拓社

ACKNOWLEDGEMENTS

The authors wish to give special thanks to the following people for their support and advice in putting the Ultimate Listening Series together:

Yuri Kamaya, Kohei Kidachi, Tetsuo Nishihara, Tsugumi Nishoji, Vince Scura, Ryan Spring, Jun Suzuki, and Matthew Wilson.

◆ 扱う英文を読み上げた音声が、開拓社ホームページからダウンロードできます。
(The audio used for this textbook can be downloaded from the Kaitakusha homepage.)

http://www.kaitakusha.co.jp/book/book.php?c=2310

◆ この本には上級編もあります。併せてご利用ください。
(*Ultimate Listening Advanced* is also available for purchase.)

『無敵リスニング〈上級〉』(Ultimate Listening〈Advanced〉)
定価 (Price):本体 1200 円＋税 (¥1200 plus tax)
ISBN978-4-7589-2311-8

Table of Contents

How do you do a dictogloss?	4
Be Active! Discussions to Build Active Learning	6
Improving Your Conversation Skills	7
Dictogloss Progress Chart	8

Stage 1 (45 words) — 9
1-1	Sunflowers	10
1-2	Making a Baseball	12
1-3	The Giraffe's Tongue	14
1-4	Barbecues in Australia	16
1-5	Walking	18

Stage 2 (55 words) — 21
2-1	Tavarua	22
2-2	Lake Hillier	24
2-3	The Orca	26
2-4	Lego-Brücke (The Lego Bridge)	28
2-5	Watermelons	30

Stage 3 (65 words) — 33
3-1	The Katakuri	34
3-2	How Tall Are You?	36
3-3	The Black Sapote: The chocolate pudding fruit	38
3-4	Japanese Festivals	40
3-5	Butterflies	42

Stage 4 (75 words) — 45
4-1	Silent Discos	46
4-2	Appian Way	48
4-3	The Sahara Desert	50
4-4	Son Doong Cave	52
4-5	Grizzly Bear	54

Stage 5 (85 words) — 57
5-1	Blueberries	58
5-2	Fortune Cookies	60
5-3	Lightning	62
5-4	Spaghetti Trees in Switzerland	64
5-5	Sleep: The 90-minute Rule	66

Stage 6 (95 words) — 69
6-1	Artificial Reefs in Mexico	70
6-2	Bananas	72
6-3	Honey	74
6-4	Rainbow Mountains in China	76
6-5	Dolphins	78

Passages and Translations	81
List of Vocabulary	91

How do you do a dictogloss?

1. Make a group of two to four people. Read the title of the passage you are going to hear. Discuss with your group members about the topic and what kind of words might appear in the passage. Share anything you know about that topic.
2. Read the first five words of the passage. Try to guess what word, or what kind of word might come next.
3. Discuss and create your strategies for doing the dictogloss with your group members.
4. Listen to the audio. Take memos of words and sentences you hear. The passage will be read quickly, so do not try to write down every word.
5. After listening to the passage once, discuss with your partner (or think alone) about what you heard and try to reconstruct as much of the passage as you can within the time limit. Look at your notes and guess words that might be in the passage.
6. Listen to the passage again and take notes.
7. With your partner, try to reconstruct the passage based on your notes. It's difficult to get 100%, so aim for 70% or higher.
8. Look at the passage (from page 81) and give yourself one point for each word you wrote correctly. Do not give yourself any points for spelling mistakes or wrong words.
9. Calculate your percentage score (the number of words you wrote correctly ÷ the total number of words x 100 (don't include the first five words)) and mark it on the progress chart. e.g., If you write 25 words of the 40 words correctly in level 1-1, you can calculate your percentage as 25 ÷ 40 x 100 = 62.5%. Numbers nine and under should be written as words, e.g., write nine, not 9. Numbers more than 10 should be written as numbers, e.g., write 10, not ten. These should be counted as one word.
10. Look at the full passage and read the passage silently as you listen to it again.
11. Read the passage aloud. For a challenge, try reading at the same speed as the native speaker.
12. Listen to the passage again without looking at your notes or the passage. Could you catch more this time?
13. Finally, write your reflection. Thinking about your performance in this dictogloss activity, what advice do you have for yourself to do better next time?

Scan the QR Code to watch a video on how to do a dictogloss.

ディクトグロスのやり方

1. 2人～4人のグループを作り、その英文のタイトルから英文の中にどんな話題、どんな英単語が出てくるかを予測し、話し合います。その際、話題について知っていることはなんでも共有しましょう。
2. 最初の5語を読み、6語目にはどんな単語が来るか推測します。
3. グループでディクトグロスの作戦について話し合います。
4. 音声を聞き、聞き取れた単語や文をメモします。読まれるスピードは速いので、文章全部を書こうとする必要はありません。
5. 一度音声を聞いたあと、グループで話し合い、設けられた時間制限の中で、英文をなるべく再現してみましょう。聞き取れなかった単語があっても、自分のメモを見て、どんな語が英文に入るかを推測します。
6. もう一度音声を聞いて、メモをとります。
7. メモをもとに、グループで文章を再現します。100%再現するのは難しいので、70%くらいを目指しましょう。
8. 巻末の英文（81ページ～）と比べてみましょう。自分がメモした単語が正しければ、それぞれに1点を与えます。スペルミスや間違った単語は0点になります。
9. 自分の正解率を計算してProgress Chartに正解率を記入します。（正しく書けた英単語の数÷総単語数×100（総単語数には最初の5個の英単語を含まない。））例えば、レベル1-1（40語）で25語が正しく書けた場合は25÷40×100 = 62.5%となります。数字の9以下の一桁の場合は英語のつづりで書きます。例えば、9はnineと書きます。10以上の二桁の数字の場合は数字表記で書きます。つまり、10は10と書いて、tenとは書きません。これらは一語にカウントされます。
10. 音声をもう一度聞きながら英文を見て黙読します。
11. 今度は、声に出して読みます。できれば、ネイティブスピーカーと同じ速さで読んでみましょう。
12. 自分のメモや英文を見ないでもう一度聞きます。今回は一回目と比べてもっと聞き取れたでしょうか。
13. 最後に自分の意見や感想を書きます。ディクトグロスで自分がどれくらいできたかを考え、次はさらに正解率が上がるように自分なりに改善点を探ってみましょう。

QR Codeをスキャンするとディクトグロスのやり方についてのビデオが見れます。

Be Active! Discussions to Build Active Learning

Active Learning has become a key word in education in recent years. Many teachers and educational institutions use 'Active Learning' as part of the goals for their courses. However, the true definition of Active Learning is not always clear. Some people think that if students are moving around the classroom, they are being active. Others regard pair work as Active Learning. In this book, we use the definition of Active Learning as provided by Grabinger and Dunlap:

> Times have changed. People now need to be able to think flexibly and creatively, solve problems, and make decisions within complex, ill-structured environments.
> (Grabinger & Dunlap, 1995, p. 27)

For us, the keywords in this definition are *flexibly*, *creatively*, *solve problems*, and *make decisions*. At the end of each dictogloss task, we have provided a discussion topic to use in your learning. There is no wrong answer or best answer for these topics. Be flexible and creative in your ideas. As you work through the book, do your best to express your opinions, listen to and respect your classmates' opinions, and think of ways to improve your English.

　近年、教育現場において、アクティブラーニングが注目されています。したがって、授業の目標にアクティブラーニングを設定する先生や教育機関が多くあります。しかし、アクティブラーニングの定義は明らかになっていない場合が多いのです。生徒が教室内を動き回っていれば、それがアクティブラーニングであると思っている人もいれば、生徒がペアワークをやっていれば、それがアクティブラーニングだと思っている人もいます。このテキストでは、グラビンジャーとダンラップという学者が提案したアクティブラーニングの定義を使用します：

> 時代が変わりました。現代の人々は頭を柔らかくし、クリエイティブな考え方を持ち、複雑で不完全な構造の環境で様々な問題を解決し課題について決断を下さなければなりません。　　　　　(Grabinger & Dunlap, 1995, p. 27)

　本テキストでは、この定義のキーワードを「頭を柔らかくする」、「クリエイティブな考え方」、「問題を解決する」や「決断を下す」とし、各ディクトグロスの最後に、ディスカッションを設けました。間違っている答えや一番良い答えはありません。頭を柔らかくしてクリエイティブな考え方でディスカッションに参加することが大切です。テキストを進める中で遠慮なく自分の意見を述べ、友だちの意見を尊重しながら聞いて、自分の英語力をどう高めるか考えてください。

Improving your Conversation Skills

How can we improve our conversations and discussions? Here are some tips to help make your conversations and discussions in the Active Learning section go better each time.

1. Try to keep the conversation going.
Rather than giving a simple answer and then passing the question on, try and make your sentence longer. For example, if the question is: 'What is your favorite season?', don't simply say 'I like summer, and you?'.
Instead try to add a comment to your answer before asking the question, like this:
'I like summer. I like summer because I like hot **weather** and I like to eat **ice cream** in summer.'
You see? You now have more topics to talk and ask about – not only summer, but also weather and ice cream!

１．会話を続ける努力をしましょう！
簡単な答えを出して質問を返すのではなく、文章を長くしてみてみましょう。たとえば、「あなたのお気に入りの季節はどれですか。」という質問がある場合は、単に「私は夏が好きです、あなたは？」と言ってはいけません。
その代わりに、次のように、質問を返す前に、自分の答えにコメントを追加してみてください：
「私は夏が好きです。私は暑い気候が好きなので夏が好きで、そして夏にアイスクリームを食べるのが好きです。」分かりましたか。今の例では話をしたり聞いたりするトピックが増えました。夏だけでなく、天気やアイスクリームも！

2. Give your opinion.
Don't be afraid of giving your opinion on a topic. Giving your opinion can make the conversation more personal.
Try using some of these phrases in your conversation to give an opinion, to agree and disagree and to ask for other people's opinions.

２．自分の意見を伝えましょう！
トピックについて意見を述べることを恐れないで下さい。自分の意見を述べることで、会話をもっと個人的なものにすることができます。あなたの会話でこれらのフレーズのいくつかを使って意見を述べ、同意し、反対し、そして他人の意見を求めましょう。

Giving your opinion 自分の意見を与える	Agreeing with someone 同意する	Disagreeing with someone 反対する	Asking for other people's opinions 他人の意見を求める
In my opinion,… As for me,…	I agree! That's a great idea!	I don't agree,… I'm not sure about that…	How about you? What do you think?
I think…	I like your suggestion!	I have a different opinion.	What ideas do you have?
How about this idea?	I think so, too.	I don't think so.	Please share your ideas.

Dictogloss Progress Chart

Color the horizontal bars to record your score.
マスに色を塗り、横の棒線で各タスクのスコア（%）を記録しよう。

Level	Date	0% ~ 9%	10% ~ 19%	20% ~ 29%	30% ~ 39%	40% ~ 49%	50% ~ 59%	60% ~ 69%	70% ~ 79%	80% ~ 89%	90% ~ 100%
1-1											
1-2											
1-3											
1-4											
1-5											
2-1											
2-2											
2-3											
2-4											
2-5											
3-1											
3-2											
3-3											
3-4											
3-5											
4-1											
4-2											
4-3											
4-4											
4-5											
5-1											
5-2											
5-3											
5-4											
5-5											
6-1											
6-2											
6-3											
6-4											
6-5											

Stage 1

Passage: 45 words
Writing time: 2 minutes

1-1 Sunflowers

GET READY

What's your favorite season? What's your *least* favorite season?

PREDICT

Discuss with a partner and write your predictions.

What do you know about the topic?	What English words do you expect to hear in the story?	What do you think the sixth word will be?
		For many people, the sunflower ...

STRATEGY TIME

What strategies are you going to use this time?

LISTEN

Scan the QR Code to hear the passage. Use this space to take memos as you listen.

RECONSTRUCT

Write the passage here. (Time: 2 minutes)

For many people, the sunflower

(/40 = %)

Remember to update your Progress Chart!

REFLECT

How can you do better next time?

ACTIVE LEARNING

Talk with your classmates about the following topics.

- What is your favorite season? With some classmates, rank summer, winter, spring, and fall into your favorite to your least favorite season. Give some reasons.

- You and your friend are planning a holiday to France. One of you wants to go in summer, the other wants to go in winter. Make a conversation to decide when you will go.

1-2 Making a Baseball

GET READY

Many people play sports to stay healthy. What do you do to stay healthy?

PREDICT

Discuss with a partner and write your predictions.

What do you know about the topic?	What English words do you expect to hear in the story?	What do you think the sixth word will be?
		In one baseball game, dozens …

STRATEGY TIME

What strategies are you going to use this time?

LISTEN

Scan the QR Code to hear the passage. Use this space to take memos as you listen.

RECONSTRUCT

Write the passage here. (Time: 2 minutes)

In one baseball game, dozens

(____ / 40 = ____ %)

Remember to update your Progress Chart!

REFLECT

How can you do better next time?

ACTIVE LEARNING

Talk with your classmates about the following topics.

- Make a new rule for baseball that would make it more interesting, more fun, more difficult, or easier (e.g., more players, bigger bats, more points for home runs).

- Imagine you have been asked to interview an American baseball fan about Japanese baseball players in the major leagues. Roleplay the interview.

1-3 The Giraffe's Tongue

GET READY

Sometimes it is difficult to decide where to go on a first date. Which do you think is better for a first date: the zoo or a movie theater?

PREDICT

Discuss with a partner and write your predictions.

What do you know about the topic?	What English words do you expect to hear in the story?	What do you think the sixth word will be?
		When you think about giraffes, ...

STRATEGY TIME

What strategies are you going to use this time?

LISTEN

Scan the QR Code to hear the passage. Use this space to take memos as you listen.

RECONSTRUCT

Write the passage here. (Time: 2 minutes)

When you think about giraffes,

_____

_____

_____

_____

_____

_____

(___ / 40 = ___ %)

Remember to update your Progress Chart!

REFLECT

How can you do better next time?

ACTIVE LEARNING

Talk with your classmates about the following topics.

- In your groups, design a zoo that would be popular with children.

- Look on the Internet at the most famous zoos in the world. Now, in pairs, roleplay a conversation in which one of you works at the famous zoo and one of you is buying tickets to go in. Talk about different tickets that are available.

1-4 Barbecues in Australia

GET READY

If your teacher visited your house for a barbeque, what would you cook?

PREDICT

Discuss with a partner and write your predictions.

What do you know about the topic?	What English words do you expect to hear in the story?	What do you think the sixth word will be?
		Australians love barbecues. You often ...

STRATEGY TIME

What strategies are you going to use this time?

LISTEN

Scan the QR Code to hear the passage. Use this space to take memos as you listen.

RECONSTRUCT

Write the passage here. (Time: 2 minutes)

Australians love barbecues. You often

_____

_____

_____

_____

_____

_____

(___ / 40 = ___ %)

Remember to update your Progress Chart!

REFLECT

How can you do better next time?

ACTIVE LEARNING

Talk with your classmates about the following topics.

- What would be the ultimate burger? In your group, think of the ingredients for the best possible hamburger and how much it would cost. Create a name for your burger.

- Many people like to eat yakisoba at barbecues in Japan. Do you think this is a good way to finish a barbecue? Have a debate with your partner about eating yakisoba at the end of a barbecue. One person agrees and one person disagrees.

1-5 Walking

GET READY

Do you prefer to take the stairs or use the elevator?

PREDICT

Discuss with a partner and write your predictions.

What do you know about the topic?	What English words do you expect to hear in the story?	What do you think the sixth word will be?
		Everyone knows that walking is ...

STRATEGY TIME

What strategies are you going to use this time?

LISTEN

Scan the QR Code to hear the passage. Use this space to take memos as you listen.

RECONSTRUCT

Write the passage here. (Time: 2 minutes)

Everyone knows that walking is

_____
_____
_____
_____
_____
_____
_____

(____ / 40 = ____ %)

Remember to update your Progress Chart!

REFLECT

How can you do better next time?

ACTIVE LEARNING

Talk with your classmates about the following topics.

- These days, pedometers, devices that count how many steps we walk, are very popular. These kinds of machines help keep us healthy. Do you use devices or applications on your smartphone to help keep you healthy?

- In pairs, imagine one of you is a walking instructor and one of you is a patient. Give advice to improve the patient's way of walking.

Stage 1 Self Report

How was your progress through Stage 1? Can you do better in Stage 2? Write a few ideas so you'll improve when you attempt the longer passages in Stage 2.

Stage 1 Vocabulary List

 Scan the QR Code to practice your vocabulary.

Word	Meaning	Level
blood pressure	血圧	1-5
body fat	体脂肪	1-5
brisk	素早い	1-5
collect	集める	1-1
cork	コルク	1-2
distance	距離	1-5
Down Under	オーストラリア	1-4
dozens of ~	数多くの～	1-2
equivalent to ~	～に相当する	1-5
feel relaxed	落ち着いた気分	1-1
gather	集まる	1-4
giraffe	キリン	1-3
good for ~	～に良い	1-5

Word	Meaning	Level
humid	蒸し暑い	1-1
lifetime	一生	1-5
neck	首	1-3
on average	平均して	1-5
plant (verb)	植える	1-1
reduce	減らす	1-5
seed	種	1-1
skin	（ボールなどの）外側	1-2
sunflower	ヒマワリ	1-1
tongue	舌	1-3
weekend	週末	1-4
yarn	糸	1-2

Stage 2

Passage: 55 words
Writing time: 2 minutes 30 seconds

2-1 Tavarua

GET READY

Do you prefer to go to the beach or go to the mountains?

PREDICT

Discuss with a partner and write your predictions.

What do you know about the topic?	What English words do you expect to hear in the story?	What do you think the sixth word will be?
		In Fiji, there is an ...

STRATEGY TIME

What strategies are you going to use this time?

LISTEN

Scan the QR Code to hear the passage. Use this space to take memos as you listen.

RECONSTRUCT

Write the passage here. (Time: 2 minutes 30 seconds)

In Fiji, there is an _____

_____

_____

_____

_____

_____

_____

(____ / 50 = ____ %)

Remember to update your Progress Chart!

REFLECT

How can you do better next time?

ACTIVE LEARNING

Talk with your classmates about the following topics.

- Mr. and Mrs. Jones have three children, aged 5, 9, and 14. They want to go on a holiday. Rank the top five places you think they should go.

- What is it like on Tavarua? Imagine you are visiting Tavarua on holiday. Roleplay a conversation with one of the local people.

2-2 Lake Hillier

GET READY

What image do you have of Australia?

PREDICT

Discuss with a partner and write your predictions.

What do you know about the topic?	What English words do you expect to hear in the story?	What do you think the sixth word will be?
		Usually, the color of lakes ...

STRATEGY TIME

What strategies are you going to use this time?

LISTEN

Scan the QR Code to hear the passage. Use this space to take memos as you listen.

RECONSTRUCT

Write the passage here. (Time: 2 minutes 30 seconds)

Usually, the color of lakes

(___ / 50 = ___ %)

Remember to update your Progress Chart!

REFLECT

How can you do better next time?

ACTIVE LEARNING

Talk with your classmates about the following topics.

- Some colors make us feel happy and some colors make us feel sad. The color of our clothes can change how we feel. What color clothes do you often wear? Do the colors of your clothes show how you feel today?

- You are organizing a camp with your friends. Decide what you need to take and who will bring each item.

2-3 The Orca

GET READY

Is it important for us to save endangered animals?

PREDICT

Discuss with a partner and write your predictions.

What do you know about the topic?	What English words do you expect to hear in the story?	What do you think the sixth word will be?
		The Orca is better known ....

STRATEGY TIME

What strategies are you going to use this time?

LISTEN

Scan the QR Code to hear the passage. Use this space to take memos as you listen.

RECONSTRUCT

Write the passage here. (Time: 2 minutes 30 seconds)

The Orca is better known

(/ 50 = %)

Remember to update your Progress Chart!

REFLECT

How can you do better next time?

ACTIVE LEARNING

Talk with your classmates about the following topics.

- Some people say animals can communicate with each other. Do you agree? Give some reasons why you agree or disagree.

- Imagine you are taking your friend to a sushi restaurant for the first time. Explain how to order sushi and any etiquette to remember at a sushi restaurant.

2-4 Lego-Brücke (The Lego Bridge)

GET READY

What are some of your earliest memories from when you were a child?

PREDICT

Discuss with a partner and write your predictions.

What do you know about the topic?	What English words do you expect to hear in the story?	What do you think the sixth word will be?
		In the city of Wuppertal ...

STRATEGY TIME

What strategies are you going to use this time?

LISTEN

Scan the QR Code to hear the passage. Use this space to take memos as you listen.

RECONSTRUCT

Write the passage here. (Time: 2 minutes 30 seconds)

In the city of Wuppertal

(/ 50 =   %)

Remember to update your Progress Chart!

REFLECT

How can you do better next time?

ACTIVE LEARNING

Talk with your classmates about the following topics.

- If you could change one thing about the design of the room you are in now, what would you change? How would that make it a better room?

- Your friend comes to your house to visit. You want to go outside to play but your friend wants to play video games inside. Roleplay the conversation.

2-5 Watermelons

GET READY

What do you think of when you hear the word "summertime?"

PREDICT

Discuss with a partner and write your predictions.

What do you know about the topic?	What English words do you expect to hear in the story?	What do you think the sixth word will be?
		In summer, nothing is more ...

STRATEGY TIME

What strategies are you going to use this time?

LISTEN

Scan the QR Code to hear the passage. Use this space to take memos as you listen.

RECONSTRUCT

Write the passage here. (Time: 2 minutes 30 seconds)

In summer, nothing is more

(/50 = %)

Remember to update your Progress Chart!

REFLECT

How can you do better next time?

ACTIVE LEARNING

Talk with your classmates about the following topics.

- In the passage, we learned that watermelons may help improve our memory. How do you memorize English words and phrases when you study?

- Make a list of 10 fruits and 10 vegetables. Then, with your partner, write a description of the difference between a fruit and a vegetable. Keep your description to less than 25 words.

Stage 2 Self Report

How was your progress through Stage 2? Can you do better in Stage 3? Write a few ideas so you'll improve when you attempt the longer passages in Stage 3.

Stage 2 Vocabulary List

 Scan the QR Code to practice your vocabulary.

Word	Meaning	Level
attract	引き寄せる	2-4
bridge	橋	2-4
dolphin	イルカ	2-3
effect	効果	2-5
hunt	狩りをする	2-3
killer whale	シャチ	2-3
lake	湖	2-2
memory	記憶	2-5
muscle pain	筋肉痛	2-5
North Pole	北極	2-3
optical illusion	錯視	2-4
orca	シャチ	2-3
reason	理由	2-2
refreshing	爽やかな	2-5
room temperature	室温	2-5
salty	しょっぱい	2-2
scientist	科学者	2-2
seal	アザラシ	2-3
shaped like ~	～の形をしている	2-1
single	独身	2-1
unique	独特の	2-4
vitamin	ビタミン	2-5
watermelon	スイカ	2-5

Stage 3

Passage: 65 words
Writing time: 3 minutes

3-1 The Katakuri

GET READY

What would you do if you received a bunch of flowers from a secret admirer?

PREDICT

Discuss with a partner and write your predictions.

What do you know about the topic?	What English words do you expect to hear in the story?	What do you think the sixth word will be?
		The katakuri is a pink ...

STRATEGY TIME

What strategies are you going to use this time?

LISTEN

Scan the QR Code to hear the passage. Use this space to take memos as you listen.

RECONSTRUCT

Write the passage here. (Time: 3 minutes)

The katakuri is a pink

(/ 60 = %)

Remember to update your Progress Chart!

REFLECT

How can you do better next time?

ACTIVE LEARNING

Talk with your classmates about the following topics.

- The katakuri is a very patient flower. It takes a long time to bloom. Are you a patient person? Tell a story about when you were very patient or very impatient.

- Find a flower shop on the Internet. Check the prices of flower delivery. Then, with your partner, roleplay a conversation ordering flowers to be delivered to your teacher.

3-2 How Tall Are You?

GET READY

How would your life be different if you were 10 centimeters taller?

PREDICT

Discuss with a partner and write your predictions.

What do you know about the topic?	What English words do you expect to hear in the story?	What do you think the sixth word will be?
		Most people know how tall ...

STRATEGY TIME

What strategies are you going to use this time?

LISTEN

Scan the QR Code to hear the passage. Use this space to take memos as you listen.

RECONSTRUCT

Write the passage here. (Time: 3 minutes)

Most people know how tall

_____

_____

_____

_____

_____

_____

_____

(___ / 60 = ___ %)

Remember to update your Progress Chart!

REFLECT

How can you do better next time?

ACTIVE LEARNING

Talk with your classmates about the following topics.

- In your opinion, what are the advantages and disadvantages of being tall? Do you want to be taller than you are now? Why?

- You have been asked to interview the tallest basketball player in the NBA. Think about what kinds of question you would ask. Roleplay the interview with your partner.

3-3 The Black Sapote: The chocolate pudding fruit

GET READY

Do you like chocolate? Talk about your favorite chocolate snack with a partner.

PREDICT

Discuss with a partner and write your predictions.

What do you know about the topic?	What English words do you expect to hear in the story?	What do you think the sixth word will be?
		There is a fruit that ...

STRATEGY TIME

What strategies are you going to use this time?

LISTEN

Scan the QR Code to hear the passage. Use this space to take memos as you listen.

RECONSTRUCT

Write the passage here. (Time: 3 minutes)

There is a fruit that _____

_____

_____

_____

_____

_____

(____ / 60 = ____ %)

Remember to update your Progress Chart!

REFLECT

How can you do better next time?

ACTIVE LEARNING

Talk with your classmates about the following topics.

- What are the most delicious fruits? In your group, then as a class, make a list of the top five most delicious fruits.

- Your group members are going to open a restaurant. Each dish on the menu includes black sapote in the ingredients. Create at least three entrées, main dishes, desserts, and drinks.

3-4 Japanese Festivals

GET READY

What traditional Japanese musical instrument would you like to learn to play?

PREDICT

Discuss with a partner and write your predictions.

What do you know about the topic?	What English words do you expect to hear in the story?	What do you think the sixth word will be?
		Japan is a country full ...

STRATEGY TIME

What strategies are you going to use this time?

LISTEN

Scan the QR Code to hear the passage. Use this space to take memos as you listen.

RECONSTRUCT

Write the passage here. (Time: 3 minutes)

Japan is a country full
_____
_____
_____
_____
_____
_____

(___ / 60 = ___ %)

Remember to update your Progress Chart!

REFLECT

How can you do better next time?

ACTIVE LEARNING

Talk with your classmates about the following topics.

- What is the best festival you have ever been to? Do you like to participate in festivals, or do you prefer to just watch?

- Japanese festivals are famous for the great variety of food sold. In your group, make a list of 10 different foods sold at festivals. Then, rank the top 5 of those foods.

3-5 Butterflies

GET READY

Some people are very interested in insects but others hate them. How do you feel about insects? Do you have a favorite insect or one you hate the most?

PREDICT

Discuss with a partner and write your predictions.

What do you know about the topic?	What English words do you expect to hear in the story?	What do you think the sixth word will be?
		Butterflies have wings and that ...

STRATEGY TIME

What strategies are you going to use this time?

LISTEN

Scan the QR Code to hear the passage. Use this space to take memos as you listen.

RECONSTRUCT

Write the passage here. (Time: 3 minutes)

Butterflies have wings and that
_____
_____
_____
_____
_____
_____

(____ / 60 = ____ %)

Remember to update your Progress Chart!

REFLECT

How can you do better next time?

[ ]

ACTIVE LEARNING

Scan the QR Code to hear the passage. Use this space to take memos as you listen.

- Scientists say that in the near future, it may become common for us to eat insects. What do you think about this? What insects do you think you *could* eat? What insects do you think you definitely could not eat?

- The idea of the Butterfly Effect suggests that everything we do affects the future. In your groups, write two stories: one in which you came to class today, and the other in which you did not come to class today. How do the two stories differ?

Stage 3 Self Report

How was your progress through Stage 3? Can you do better in Stage 4? Write a few ideas so you'll improve when you attempt the longer passages in Stage 4.

Stage 3 Vocabulary List

Scan the QR Code to practice your vocabulary.

Word	Meaning	Level	Word	Meaning	Level
attractive	魅力的	3-5	instead of ~	~の代わりに	3-3
bloom	咲く	3-1	participant	参加者	3-4
bulb	球根	3-1	persimmon	柿	3-3
butterfly	蝶	3-5	repel	はじく	3-5
celebrate	祝う	3-4	spine	背骨	3-2
delicious	美味しい	3-4	stall	屋台	3-4
dirt	汚れ	3-5	such as	例えば	3-1
dream	夢	3-3	taste like ~	~のような味がする	3-3
due to ~	~による	3-2	a variety of ~	様々な~	3-4
festival	祭り	3-4	waterproof	防水	3-5
fluid	液体	3-2	wing	羽	3-5
gravity	重力	3-2			

Stage 4

Passage: 75 words
Writing time: 3 minutes 30 seconds

4-1 Silent Discos

GET READY

Do you enjoy dancing?

PREDICT

Discuss with a partner and write your predictions.

What do you know about the topic?	What English words do you expect to hear in the story?	What do you think the sixth word will be?
		Many people love discos. They ...

STRATEGY TIME

What strategies are you going to use this time?

LISTEN

Scan the QR Code to hear the passage. Use this space to take memos as you listen.

RECONSTRUCT

Write the passage here. (Time: 3 minutes 30 seconds)

Many people love discos. They

(/ 70 = %)

Remember to update your Progress Chart!

REFLECT

How can you do better next time?

ACTIVE LEARNING

Talk with your classmates about the following topics.

- Discos are popular with young people. However, do you think someone can be too old to go to a disco where there are many young people? In your group, decide an age for men and women that might be considered too old to go to a disco.

- Imagine you are studying on the train. The person sitting next to you is wearing earphones and listening to music. However, the music is so loud you can hear it. Roleplay a conversation with the person.

4-2 Appian Way

GET READY

Do you like to visit museums when you travel somewhere new?

PREDICT

Discuss with a partner and write your predictions.

What do you know about the topic?	What English words do you expect to hear in the story?	What do you think the sixth word will be?
		There is a famous phrase ...

STRATEGY TIME

What strategies are you going to use this time?

LISTEN

Scan the QR Code to hear the passage. Use this space to take memos as you listen.

RECONSTRUCT

Write the passage here. (Time: 3 minutes 30 seconds)

There is a famous phrase

_____

_____

_____

_____

_____

_____

_____

_____

(_____ / 70 = _____ %)

Remember to update your Progress Chart!

REFLECT

How can you do better next time?

ACTIVE LEARNING

Talk with your classmates about the following topics.

- Is it important to study about world history? Share your opinion with your group members and the class.

- Imagine you could have dinner with any person in history. Roleplay a conversation with that person.

4-3 The Sahara Desert

GET READY

Do you prefer hot weather or cold weather?

PREDICT

Discuss with a partner and write your predictions.

What do you know about the topic?	What English words do you expect to hear in the story?	What do you think the sixth word will be?
		If you ever feel hot ...

STRATEGY TIME

What strategies are you going to use this time?

LISTEN

Scan the QR Code to hear the passage. Use this space to take memos as you listen.

RECONSTRUCT

Write the passage here. (Time: 3 minutes 30 seconds)

If you ever feel hot

(/ 70 = %)

Remember to update your Progress Chart!

REFLECT

How can you do better next time?

ACTIVE LEARNING

Talk with your classmates about the following topics.

- Imagine you had to spend one year on a desert island. What is one thing you would take with you? (Of course, you are provided with water, food, and shelter.)

- Find some information on the Internet about tours of the Sahara. Roleplay a conversation booking a holiday in the Sahara. Decide on some optional tours.

4-4 Son Doong Cave

GET READY

What image do you have of Vietnam?

PREDICT

Discuss with a partner and write your predictions.

What do you know about the topic?	What English words do you expect to hear in the story?	What do you think the sixth word will be?
		In Vietnam, there is a ...

STRATEGY TIME

What strategies are you going to use this time?

LISTEN

Scan the QR Code to hear the passage. Use this space to take memos as you listen.

52

RECONSTRUCT

Write the passage here. (Time: 3 minutes 30 seconds)

In Vietnam, there is a

(/ 70 = %)

Remember to update your Progress Chart!

REFLECT

How can you do better next time?

ACTIVE LEARNING

Talk with your classmates about the following topics.

- Are you interested in visiting other countries and seeing unusual places there? Do you think you could ever live in another country?

- Find a menu for a Vietnamese restaurant. Roleplay a conversation ordering food and drinks at the restaurant.

4-5 Grizzly Bear

GET READY

Have you ever seen a bear in the wild? What would you do if you saw one?

PREDICT

Discuss with a partner and write your predictions.

What do you know about the topic?	What English words do you expect to hear in the story?	What do you think the sixth word will be?
		One of the most popular ….

STRATEGY TIME

What strategies are you going to use this time?

LISTEN

Scan the QR Code to hear the passage. Use this space to take memos as you listen.

RECONSTRUCT

Write the passage here. (Time: 3 minutes 30 seconds)

One of the most popular _____

_____

_____

_____

_____

_____

_____

_____

(____ / 70 = ____ %)

Remember to update your Progress Chart!

REFLECT

How can you do better next time?

ACTIVE LEARNING

Talk with your classmates about the following topics.

- What dangerous animals do you know? Make a ranking of what you think are the top five most dangerous land and sea animals in the world.

- Some people hunt bears as a sport. What do you think about hunting? Roleplay a conversation between you and a hunter about the sport.

Stage 4 Self Report

How was your progress through Stage 4? Can you do better in Stage 5? Write a few ideas so you'll improve when you attempt the longer passages in Stage 5.

Stage 4 Vocabulary List

Scan the QR Code to practice your vocabulary.

Word	Meaning	Level	Word	Meaning	Level
actually	実際に	4-3	moose	ヘラジカ	4-5
aggressive	攻撃的な	4-5	nearby	近くに	4-1
Arabic	アラビア語	4-3	phrase	ことわざ	4-2
army	軍隊	4-2	plant (noun)	植物	4-5
bitterly cold	非常に寒い	4-3	protective	保護的な	4-5
can't ~ a thing	一つも出来ない	4-1	rain forest	熱帯雨林	4-4
cave	洞窟	4-4	Roman Empire	ローマ帝国	4-2
cub	小熊	4-5	severe	厳しい	4-3
defend	守る	4-5	soft toy	ぬいぐるみ	4-5
desert	砂漠	4-3	spare a thought for ~	～のことを少し考える	4-3
enjoy ~ing	～をするのを楽しむ	4-1	strategically	戦略的に	4-2
extremely	極めて	4-3	thirsty	喉が渇いた	4-3
~ in itself	～だけで	4-2	transmit	送る	4-1

Stage 5

Passage: 85 words
Writing time: 4 minutes

5-1 Blueberries

GET READY

What fruits do you think are the most delicious?

PREDICT

Discuss with a partner and write your predictions.

What do you know about the topic?	What English words do you expect to hear in the story?	What do you think the sixth word will be?
		Blueberries are very popular. They ...

STRATEGY TIME

What strategies are you going to use this time?

LISTEN

Scan the QR Code to hear the passage. Use this space to take memos as you listen.

58

RECONSTRUCT

Write the passage here. (Time: 4 minutes)

Blueberries are very popular. They

(/ 80 = %)

Remember to update your Progress Chart!

REFLECT

How can you do better next time?

ACTIVE LEARNING

Talk with your classmates about the following topics.

- Sometimes, it can be hard to grow berries or other fruit and vegetables at your own home. But this can also be very rewarding. Do you want to grow your own food or buy frozen fruit and vegetables from the supermarket? Share your opinion and give some reasons.

- Try having a debate with your partner. The topic is, "It is better to be a blueberry than it is to be human."

5-2 Fortune Cookies

GET READY

Do you often eat Chinese food?

PREDICT

Discuss with a partner and write your predictions.

What do you know about the topic?	What English words do you expect to hear in the story?	What do you think the sixth word will be?
		If you go out for ...

STRATEGY TIME

What strategies are you going to use this time?

LISTEN

Scan the QR Code to hear the passage. Use this space to take memos as you listen.

RECONSTRUCT

Write the passage here. (Time: 4 minutes)

If you go out for

_____

_____

_____

_____

_____

_____

_____

(/ 80 =   %)

Remember to update your Progress Chart!

REFLECT

How can you do better next time?

ACTIVE LEARNING

Talk with your classmates about the following topics.

- How many different ways of telling someone's personality can you think of (e.g., star sign, blood type, etc.)? Do you believe in these? Why or why not?

- Roleplay a conversation between you and a fortune teller.

5-3 Lightning

GET READY

What can we do to help the environment?

PREDICT

Discuss with a partner and write your predictions.

What do you know about the topic?	What English words do you expect to hear in the story?	What do you think the sixth word will be?
		Very strong sudden bursts of ...

STRATEGY TIME

What strategies are you going to use this time?

LISTEN

Scan the QR Code to hear the passage. Use this space to take memos as you listen.

RECONSTRUCT

Write the passage here. (Time: 4 minutes)

Very strong sudden bursts of _____

_____

_____

_____

_____

_____

_____

(_____ / 80 = _____%)

Remember to update your Progress Chart!

REFLECT

How can you do better next time?

ACTIVE LEARNING

Talk with your classmates about the following topics.

- What is the hottest and/or coldest weather that you have ever experienced? Where and when was it? What did it feel like?

- Find a weather map for a foreign country. Give a weather forecast for that country.

5-4 Spaghetti Trees in Switzerland

GET READY

Have you ever played a practical joke on someone? Have you ever seen one on television?

PREDICT

Discuss with a partner and write your predictions.

What do you know about the topic?	What English words do you expect to hear in the story?	What do you think the sixth word will be?
		In 1957, the BBC, a ...

STRATEGY TIME

What strategies are you going to use this time?

LISTEN

Scan the QR Code to hear the passage. Use this space to take memos as you listen.

RECONSTRUCT

Write the passage here. (Time: 4 minutes)

In 1957, the BBC, a

(/ 80 = %)

Remember to update your Progress Chart!

REFLECT

How can you do better next time?

ACTIVE LEARNING

Talk with your classmates about the following topics.

- There are many different kinds of noodles: ramen, soba, udon, somen, and spaghetti. In your groups, rank these noodles in order from your favorite to least favorite.

- The day after the spaghetti tree hoax, many people called the BBC to ask about spaghetti trees. Roleplay a phone call between someone who saw the story about spaghetti trees on television and someone working at the BBC.

5-5 Sleep: The 90-minute Rule

GET READY

Some people say it is not healthy for us to use phones or computers before going to bed. Do you use your phone before going to bed?

PREDICT

Discuss with a partner and write your predictions.

What do you know about the topic?	What English words do you expect to hear in the story?	What do you think the sixth word will be?
		A sleep expert from England ...

STRATEGY TIME

What strategies are you going to use this time?

LISTEN

Scan the QR Code to hear the passage. Use this space to take memos as you listen.

RECONSTRUCT

Write the passage here. (Time: 4 minutes)

A sleep expert from England

(/ 80 = %)

Remember to update your Progress Chart!

REFLECT

How can you do better next time?

ACTIVE LEARNING

Talk with your classmates about the following topics.

- About how many hours do you sleep every night? Do you have trouble waking up in the morning? In your opinion, what is the best way to wake up feeling refreshed in the morning?

- You are going to organize to meet your friend one morning to study for a test. However, your friend often sleeps in and is late. Make a conversation with your partner to make sure you meet on time.

Stage 5 Self Report

How was your progress through Stage 5? Can you do better in Stage 6? Write a few ideas so you'll improve when you attempt the longer passages in Stage 6.

Stage 5 Vocabulary List

 Scan the QR Code to practice your vocabulary.

Word	Meaning	Level	Word	Meaning	Level
biscuit	ビスケット	5-2	invent	発明する	5-2
broadcast	放送する	5-4	lightning strike	落雷	5-3
burst	突発	5-3	micro~	100万分の1	5-3
count back	逆から数える	5-5	nutrient	栄養	5-1
cycle	周期	5-5	pray	祈る	5-4
electricity	電気	5-3	state	状態	5-5
exist	存在する	5-4	strike	（雷が）落ちる	5-3
expert	専門家	5-5	sudden	突然の	5-3
feel refreshed	気持ち良い	5-5	suggest	提案する	5-5
fortune cookie	おみくじ入りクッキー	5-2	Switzerland	スイス	5-4
hoax	悪ふざけ	5-4	thunderstorm	嵐	5-3
intend	目指す	5-1	Venezuela	ベネズエラ	5-3

Stage 6

Passage: 95 words
Writing time: 4 minutes 30 seconds

6-1 Artificial Reefs in Mexico

GET READY

How do you tell the difference between real and fake items?

PREDICT

Discuss with a partner and write your predictions.

What do you know about the topic?	What English words do you expect to hear in the story?	What do you think the sixth word will be?
		Off the east coast of ...

STRATEGY TIME

What strategies are you going to use this time?

LISTEN

Scan the QR Code to hear the passage. Use this space to take memos as you listen.

RECONSTRUCT

Write the passage here. (Time: 4 minutes 30 seconds)

Off the east coast of

_____

_____

_____

_____

_____

_____

_____

(/ 90 =   %)

Remember to update your Progress Chart!

REFLECT

How can you do better next time?

ACTIVE LEARNING

Talk with your classmates about the following topics.

- Think of some places in your town that need to be cleaned up or changed in some way. What ideas do you have to clean up or change those places and make them more attractive for visitors?

- You and your friends are planning a week of diving off the coast of Mexico. Make plans with a travel agent for the trip.

6-2 Bananas

GET READY

Bananas give us energy. What do you do when you need some energy?

PREDICT

Discuss with a partner and write your predictions.

What do you know about the topic?	What English words do you expect to hear in the story?	What do you think the sixth word will be?
		Bananas are one of the ...

STRATEGY TIME

What strategies are you going to use this time?

LISTEN

Scan the QR Code to hear the passage. Use this space to take memos as you listen.

RECONSTRUCT

Write the passage here. (Time: 4 minutes 30 seconds)

Bananas are one of the

(/ 90 = %)

Remember to update your Progress Chart!

REFLECT

How can you do better next time?

ACTIVE LEARNING

Talk with your classmates about the following topics.

- Make a menu for a restaurant that has banana in everything on the menu. Make sure you have some variety and include at least three entrées, main dishes, desserts, and drinks on your menu. Finally, give your restaurant a name.

- Smoothie bars are popular in many countries. Look on the Internet for menus from smoothie bars around the world. Then, roleplay a conversation ordering two smoothies with extra toppings.

6-3 Honey

GET READY

Do you have a sweet tooth?

PREDICT

Discuss with a partner and write your predictions.

What do you know about the topic?	What English words do you expect to hear in the story?	What do you think the sixth word will be?
		If you have a sweet ...

STRATEGY TIME

What strategies are you going to use this time?

LISTEN

Scan the QR Code to hear the passage. Use this space to take memos as you listen.

RECONSTRUCT

Write the passage here. (Time: 4 minutes 30 seconds)

If you have a sweet

(/ 90 = %)

Remember to update your Progress Chart!

REFLECT

How can you do better next time?

ACTIVE LEARNING

Talk with your classmates about the following topics.

- Do you think your teacher likes sweet food? Make a list of what you think your teacher's three favorite sweet foods are. Check to see if you were right.

- Honey doesn't have a use by date, but many foods do. Roleplay a conversation, in which your friend is going to eat a biscuit which has passed its use-by date by one month.

6-4 Rainbow Mountains in China

GET READY

What image do you have of China?

PREDICT

Discuss with a partner and write your predictions.

What do you know about the topic?	What English words do you expect to hear in the story?	What do you think the sixth word will be?
		Zhangye Danxia Landform Geological Park ...

STRATEGY TIME

What strategies are you going to use this time?

LISTEN

Scan the QR Code to hear the passage. Use this space to take memos as you listen.

RECONSTRUCT

Write the passage here. (Time: 4 minutes 30 seconds)

Zhangye Danxia Landform Geological Park

_____

_____

_____

_____

_____

_____

_____

_____

(___ / 90 = ___ %)

Remember to update your Progress Chart!

REFLECT

How can you do better next time?

ACTIVE LEARNING

Talk with your classmates about the following topics.

- Create a one-minute television-style commercial to persuade people to visit your town. Make it entertaining with some humor and use pictures so people will want to come.

- Find out how to say some phrases in Chinese. Teach your group members some Chinese phrases and try to have a simple conversation.

6-5 Dolphins

GET READY

Do you prefer beef or fish?

PREDICT

Discuss with a partner and write your predictions.

What do you know about the topic?	What English words do you expect to hear in the story?	What do you think the sixth word will be?
		It is common knowledge that …

STRATEGY TIME

What strategies are you going to use this time?

LISTEN

Scan the QR Code to hear the passage. Use this space to take memos as you listen.

RECONSTRUCT

Write the passage here. (Time: 4 minutes 30 seconds)

It is common knowledge that

(/ 90 = %)

Remember to update your Progress Chart!

REFLECT

How can you do better next time?

ACTIVE LEARNING

Talk with your classmates about the following topics.

- Many people say dolphins are very intelligent animals. Which are the most intelligent, though? In groups of three or four, make a list of the five most intelligent animals (including humans!).

- Imagine you could have a conversation with a dolphin. What kinds of things would you talk about? Roleplay a conversation between you and a dolphin.

Stage 6 Self Report

How was your progress through Stage 6? Did you feel your listening skills improved throughout this book? What listening strategies did you learn?

Stage 6 Vocabulary List

 Scan the QR Code to practice your vocabulary.

Word	Meaning	Level	Word	Meaning	Level
agility	軽快さ	6-5	heart attack	心臓発作	6-2
alien	地球上のものでない	6-4	install	設置する	6-1
ancient	古代の	6-3	liquid	液体	6-5
artificial	人工的	6-1	mineral	鉱物	6-4
blowhole	噴水孔	6-5	Mother Nature	母なる自然	6-3
classification	分類	6-2	mountain range	山脈	6-4
classify	分類する	6-2	off the coast	沖に	6-1
coral reef	サンゴ礁	6-1	sandstone	砂岩	6-4
cure	治療	6-3	sculpture	彫刻	6-1
deposit	堆積	6-4	source	源	6-2
drown	溺れる	6-5	spooky	不気味	6-1
encourage	促す	6-1	stroke	脳卒中	6-2
energetic	エネルギッシュ	6-2	stunning	極めて美しい	6-4
estimate	推測する	6-2	sweet tooth	甘党である	6-3
exotic	エキゾチックな	6-4	use by date	消費期限	6-3
heal	治す	6-3	wound	傷	6-3

Passages and Translations

1-1 Sunflowers （ヒマワリ）
For many people, the sunflower is a symbol of summer. Their bright yellow colors make us feel relaxed on hot, humid summer days. At the end of summer, you can collect the seeds to plant the next year, or eat them as a healthy snack.

多くの人にとって、ヒマワリは夏のシンボルだ。蒸し暑い夏の日にそれらの鮮やかな黄色が私たちをリラックスさせる。夏の終わりには種を集め、次の年に植える、またはヘルシーなおやつにもなる。

1-2 Making a Baseball （野球ボールの作り方）
In one baseball game, dozens of balls may be used. Have you ever thought about what these balls are made of? Each ball has cork in the center. Around this there is yarn or even wool. Finally, a leather skin is put on the outside.

野球一試合の中で、無数のボールが使われるかもしれない。これらのボールは何で作られているかを考えたことがある？ボールの中心部はコルクで、その外側を糸、そして毛系で巻く。一番外側に革が張られている。

1-3 The Giraffe's Tongue （キリンの舌）
When you think about giraffes, you probably think about their long necks. But did you know that giraffes have long tongues, too? Giraffes' tongues can be up to 50 centimeters long. This is so long, it means giraffes can clean their ears with their tongues!

キリンについて考える時、長い首をイメージするだろう。でも、キリンの舌も長いことは知っていた？キリンの舌は約５０センチメートルもの長さである。こんなに長いからこそキリンは舌で自分の耳を掃除できるんだ！

1-4 Barbecues in Australia （オーストラリアでのバーベキュー）
Australians love barbecues. You often see families and friends gather at home, a park, or the beach to have barbecue lunches on weekends in summer. Eating steak, sausages, and pineapple grilled on the barbecue together with some salad makes for a great day Down Under.

オーストラリア人はバーベキューが大好き。家、公園、またビーチなどで多くの家族や友人たちが夏の週末にバーベキューの昼食をするために集まっているのがよく見られる。サラダと一緒にバーベキューで焼いたステーキ、ソーセージ、パイナップルを食べることでダウンアンダー（オーストラリア）での一日が素晴らしいものになる。

1-5 Walking （歩くこと）
Everyone knows that walking is good for our health. Going for brisk walks not only helps reduce body fat and lower blood pressure, but makes us feel happy, too. On average, humans walk the equivalent distance of three times around the world in a lifetime.

歩くことが健康に良いとみんな知っているだろう。素早く歩くと、体脂肪を減らしたり血圧を下げたりするだけでなく、気分が良くなる。平均して、人間は生きている間に世界の３周分に相当する距離を歩くと言われている。

2-1 Tavarua （タヴァルア）
In Fiji, there is an island that is shaped like a heart. It is called Tavarua. The island is used as a resort and many people visit Tavarua to surf, fish, play beach volleyball, go diving, or just relax. Tavarua is the perfect place for holidays and is popular for singles, couples, and families alike.

フィジーには、ハートのような形をした島がある。タヴァルアと呼ばれている。その島はリゾート地として利用されており、多くの人がタヴァルアを訪れ、サーフィンをしたり、釣りをしたり、ビーチバレーをしたり、ダイビングをしたり、ただリラックスしたりする。タヴァルアは休暇にはうってつけの場所で、一人旅やカップル、また家族連れにも人気がある。

2-2 Lake Hillier （ヒリアー湖）
Usually, the color of lakes is blue, green, or brown. However, there is a lake in Western Australia that is pink. Lake Hillier doesn't look a little pink, but very pink, like bubble gum. Scientists aren't sure why it is pink, but the water is very salty and this may be one of the reasons.

大概、湖の色は青か、緑か茶色だ。しかし、西オーストラリアにはピンク色をした湖が存在する。ヒリアー湖はちょっとピンク色に見えるというわけではなく、本当にピンク色なのだ、風船ガムみたいに。科学者は、なぜピンクなのか定かではないが、湖の水がとてもしょっぱいことから、このことが理由の一つだろうと考えている。

2-3 The Orca （シャチ）
The Orca is better known as the Killer Whale. It is black and white and the largest of the dolphins. Orcas usually live in cold areas, such as near the North Pole. They eat other sea animals, for example seals and even whales. Orcas usually travel and hunt in family groups of about forty members.

シャチは「キラーホエール」としてよく知られている。体は白黒でイルカの中で一番大きい。シャチはたいてい北極に近い地域のような寒い地域に住んでいる。そこでアザラシや鯨などの海獣を食べている。シャチは普段は４０頭ほどの家族の群れで移動し捕食している。

2-4 Lego-Brücke (The Lego Bridge) （レゴの橋）
In the city of Wuppertal, Germany, an artist painted one of the bridges giving it an optical illusion. It now looks like it was made of Lego blocks. It took the artist four weeks to paint the bridge, changing it from a boring, grey, concrete bridge, to a unique, colorful one that attracts many visitors.

ドイツのヴッパタール町で、画家がある橋を錯視に見えるように色を塗った。その橋は、レゴブロックでできているように見える。画家はその橋を塗り上げるのに４週間費やし、ぱっとしない灰色のコンクリートの橋を変え、多くの観光客を魅了するユニークでカラフルなものにしたのだ。

2-5 Watermelons （スイカ）

In summer, nothing is more refreshing than a nice, juicy watermelon. But did you know that watermelons do much more than cool you down? Watermelons contain many vitamins curing muscle pain and even improving memory. When you eat a watermelon, make sure it is not too cold, but at room temperature for the best effects.

夏、おいしくみずみずしいスイカほどリフレッシュできるものはない。しかしあなたは、スイカがクールダウン以上のことをしてくれることをご存じだろうか。スイカは筋肉痛を治したり、そして記憶力も良くしてくれるビタミンを多く含んでいるのだ。スイカを食べるときはスイカを冷やしすぎず、一番効果が期待できるよう、室温にすることを忘れずに。

3-1 The Katakuri （カタクリ）

The katakuri is a pink flower found in Japan and other countries of Asia, such as Korea, northeastern China, and east Russia. It is usually about twenty centimeters high and blooms in forests from April through to June. A katakuri grows slowly, and it can take more than seven years before bulbs are ready to flower. Some people use the bulbs for starch in cooking.

カタクリとは日本や韓国、中国東北部、ロシア東部などの他のアジアの国で見られるピンクの花だ。たいていは背丈約２０㎝で４月から６月にかけて森で花を咲かせる。カタクリはゆっくり成長し、球根が花を咲かせるまでに実に７年以上を費やす。その球根を料理の際に片栗粉として利用する人もいる。

3-2 How Tall Are You? （あなたの身長は何センチ？）

Most people know how tall they are. However, did you know you are a little taller in the morning than you are in the evening? Scientists say that this might be because of extra fluid that gathers around the spine when we sleep. This is then lost during the day due to gravity. If you want to stay taller during the day, try doing yoga.

ほとんどの人は自分の身長を知っている。でも、夕方より朝の方が身長が高いと知っていた？研究者によるとその理由は寝ている間に背骨に液体がたまるからだ。そして、日中には重力の影響でこの液体がなくなる。日中に背の高い状態をキープにしたかったらヨガをやってみよう。

3-3 The Black Sapote - The chocolate pudding fruit
（ブラックサポテ：チョコレートプリン味の果物）

There is a fruit that tastes like chocolate pudding. On the outside, black sapotes look a bit like persimmons. However, the inside is black. They are very healthy with four times as much vitamin C as oranges. Because they are low in fat, black sapotes are sometimes used instead of chocolate in milkshakes. If you like chocolate, the black sapote is a dream come true!

チョコレートプリン味の果物がある。ブラックサポテの外側は柿に似ている。しかし、中は黒。オレンジの４倍分のビタミンＣを含み、ブラックサポテはとても体にいい。低脂肪のため、ブラックサポテは時にはチョコレートの代わりにミルクシェイクに使われることもある。チョコレートが好きであれば、ブラックサポテは夢のような果物だ。

3-4 Japanese Festivals （日本の祭り）

Japan is a country full of interesting and unusual festivals. A popular time of the year to have a festival is fall. Participants in these festivals often play Japanese drums, dance, and sing to celebrate the rice harvest. At these fall festivals, there are many stalls. At these stalls, you can buy a variety of delicious festival food, such as fried noodles and chocolate bananas.

日本は面白くて変わった祭りでいっぱいの国だ。一年のうち、祭りが多く開催されるのは秋だ。参加者は祭りで和太鼓をたたき、五穀豊穣を祝うために歌って踊る。このような秋祭りには、たくさんの出店がある。これらの出店では、焼きそばやチョコバナナなどの様々な種類のおいしいお祭りフードが買える。

3-5 Butterflies （蝶）

Butterflies have wings and that is why they can fly, of course. However, these wings are not only beautiful but also waterproof. The wings of a butterfly can repel both water and dirt. This keeps their wings dry, making it easier for them to fly. It also makes them attractive to other butterflies. Scientists are studying the wings of butterflies to create clean, waterproof materials.

蝶は羽があり、もちろん、だから飛べるのだ。しかしながら、蝶の羽は美しいだけではなく、水を通さないのだ。蝶の羽は水も汚れもはじくことができる。これは羽を常に乾いた状態に保ち、より楽に飛べるようにしている。また他の蝶を引きつける。清潔で水をはじく物質を作るために、蝶の羽を研究する科学者もいる。

4-1 Silent Discos （サイレント・ディスコ）

Many people love discos. They go to listen to music, dance, and have fun with friends. However, one of the problems with discos is the loud noise. Many people who live nearby complain that the music is too loud. To overcome this, silent discos are becoming more popular. People at the discos wear headphones and the music is transmitted through these. People outside can't hear a thing, but inside everyone enjoys dancing to the music.

多くの人はディスコが大好きだ。音楽を聴き、踊り、友達と楽しく過ごす。しかし、ディスコの問題の一つが騒音だ。近くに住む多くの人が音楽がうるさすぎると苦情を言う。これを克服するべく、サイレント・ディスコが普及しつつある。ディスコにいる人はイヤフォンを装着し、音楽はそこから流れる。外の人たちには何も聞こえないが、中にいる全員は音楽でダンスを楽しめるというわけだ。

4-2 Appian Way （アッピア街道）

There is a famous phrase in English, "All roads lead to Rome." But how about roads in Rome? For centuries, the Roman Empire had the strongest army in the world. You can experience those times at Appian Way, the oldest road in Rome. The first part of Appian Way was completed 2300 years ago and was a strategically important point for the Roman army. Now, walking along Appian Way is a history lesson in itself.

英語には「すべての道はローマに通ず」という有名な諺がある。しかしローマの道はどうなのだろう？何世紀にもわたって、ローマ帝国には世界で最強の軍隊がいた。その時代をローマ最古の道アッピア街道で体験することができる。アッピア街道の初めの部分は２３００年前に完成し、ローマ軍の戦略上重要な場所のひとつであった。今となっては、現在ローマではアッピア街道を歩くことが歴史の授業の一環になっている。

4-3 The Sahara Desert （サハラ砂漠）

If you ever feel hot or thirsty, spare a thought for those in the Sahara Desert. The Sahara Desert is the world's largest desert. It has some of the most severe weather on Earth with almost no rain, strong wind, and temperatures that range from extremely hot during the day to bitterly cold at night. In Arabic, the word *sahara* actually means desert. So when you say Sahara Desert, you are actually saying, "Desert Desert."

今まで暑さやのどの渇きを感じたことがあるなら、サハラ砂漠でそんなことが起きたらと考えてみよ。サハラ砂漠は世界で一番大きな砂漠だ。そこは地球上もっとも過酷な天候を有しており、ほとんど雨が降らず、風が強く、そして気温差は日中も尋常じゃないほどに暑く、夜は体が痛いほど寒い。アラビア語で「サハラ」という言葉は、実は「砂漠」という意味である。だから「サハラ砂漠」と言えば、実際には「砂漠砂漠」と言っていることになる。

4-4 Son Doong Cave （ソンドン洞）

In Vietnam, there is a big cave. In fact, it's enormous. Son Doong Cave is the world's largest cave. However, despite it being so big, it wasn't discovered until 1991. The cave is more than five kilometers long, 200 meters high, and 150 meters wide. Inside, there is a river and even a rain forest. There are cave tours, but it will take you more than a day to get there from the nearest towns.

ベトナムに、大きな洞窟がある。実は、巨大だ。ソンドン洞は世界一大きい洞窟だ。しかし、そんなに大きいにもかかわらず、１９９１年まで発見されていなかった。その洞窟は全長５ｋｍ以上、高さ２００ｍ、幅１５０ｍもある。中には、川やはたまた熱帯雨林までもが存在する。洞窟ツアーがあるが、そこにたどり着くだけでも最寄りの町から１日以上かかってしまうだろう。

4-5 Grizzly Bear （ハイイログマ）

One of the most popular soft toy animals for children is the bear. However, a real bear is much more dangerous than the one many of us took to bed as a child. Grizzly bears can grow more than two meters long and weigh 350 kilograms. They eat plants and meat such as salmon, moose, and deer. Grizzly bears are protective and can be very aggressive to anyone, including humans, when defending their young cubs.

子供たちに最も人気のあるぬいぐるみのひとつと言えばクマだ。しかし本当のクマは、私たちの多くが子供の頃、ベッドにもっていったクマよりずっと危ない。ハイイログマは体長２ｍ以上、体重３５０kgに成長しうる。植物や、そしてサケ、ムース（ヘラジカ）、シカといった肉を食べる。ハイイログマは何かを守る習性があり、人間を含む動物に攻撃的になることがあるが、それは子グマを守ろうとするときである。

5-1 Blueberries （ブルーベリー）

Blueberries are very popular. They are probably one of the most loved of the berry family. Not only do they taste delicious, they are also very good for you. Did you know eating blueberries can help you lose weight, stay looking young, and improve your memory? They also make you feel happier. There are many ways of eating blueberries, such as in muffins, cakes, and cookies. However, the best way to enjoy their flavor and nutrients is the way nature intended, straight off the bush.

ブルーベリーはとても人気がある。おそらく最も人気のあるベリーの一つだ。おいしいだけでなく、あなたにとってもいいものなのだ。ブルーベリーを食べると体重を減らしたり、見た目の若さを保ったり、記憶力を向上させるのに役立つかもしれないと知っていた？そして幸せな気分にもしてくれるのだ。ブルーベリーの食べ方はたくさんある、マフィンに、ケーキやクッキーの中に、といった感じで。しかし、味と栄養素を満喫する一番いい方法は、自然のままで、畑から直接きたものをいただくことだ。

5-2 Fortune Cookies （フォーチュンクッキー）

If you go out for Chinese food in a Western country, you might be given a fortune cookie at the end of your meal. Fortune cookies are biscuits given as part of dessert and have a short message written on a piece of paper inside. Even though they are usually eaten with Chinese food, some people say the fortune cookie was actually invented by an American man around the year 1920. Other people think the fortune cookie was invented in Japan about 50 years earlier.

欧米では中華料理店に行くと、食事の最後にフォーチュンクッキー（おみくじ入りクッキー）が出てくることがある。フォーチュンクッキーはデザートの一部で、中に短いメッセージの書いてある小さい紙が入っている。普段、中華料理店で食べられているのだが、フォーチュンクッキーは１９２０年前後にアメリカ人によって発明されたと言う人もいる。さらに、それより５０年も前に日本で発明されたという説もある。

5-3 Lightning （落雷）

Very strong sudden bursts of electricity during a thunderstorm are better known as lightning. A lightning strike lasts only one or two microseconds with a temperature of about 20000 degrees Celsius. Most lightning strikes happen on land, not over the ocean. Although it is said that lightning never strikes in the same place twice, there is a place in Venezuela that has lightning storms 160 days a year. During a lightning storm there, there can be up to 280 lightning strikes in just one hour!

嵐の時に起こる突然の非常に強い放電は落雷として知られている。落雷の温度は２００００℃で、１００万分の１秒か２秒で終わる。ほとんどの落雷は海の上ではなく陸の上で起こる。落雷は同じ場所に二度と起こらないと言われているが、ベネズエラのとあるところでは年間１６０日も落雷が発生する。そこでは一時間あたりの落雷は２８０回にも及ぶ。

5-4 Spaghetti Trees in Switzerland （スイスのスパゲティーの木）

In 1957, the BBC, a British news broadcasting network, showed a short news program about Spaghetti Trees in Switzerland. It showed videos of people picking spaghetti from trees. Of course, it was not true. It was a hoax shown on April Fool's Day. However, many people believed the story and thought that Spaghetti Trees really existed. The next day, the BBC received phone calls asking where to buy Spaghetti Trees. The BBC said, "Put a piece of spaghetti in a can of tomatoes and pray."

１９５７年にイギリスの放送局ＢＢＣがスイスのスパゲティーの木についての短いニュースを放送した。人々が木からスパゲティーを収穫している映像もあった。もちろんこのニュースは嘘だった。４月１日のエイプリルフールに合わせて放送した作り話だった。しかし、これは本当の話だと信じていた人が多く、スパゲティーの木が存在すると思った。その次の日にスパゲティーの木はどこで買えるかとＢＢＣに電話した人も多くいた。ＢＢＣからの返答は「トマトの缶詰にスパゲティーを一本植えて祈ってください」。

5-5 Sleep: The 90-minute Rule （睡眠：９０分ルール）

A sleep expert from England suggests that to wake up in the morning feeling refreshed, we should carefully calculate the time we need to go to bed by counting back in groups of 90 minutes from the time we want to wake up. Humans sleep in 90-minute cycles. After 90 minutes, we return to a state closest to that of when we are awake. So, to wake up feeling fresh at six o'clock, it's better to go to bed at 12 o'clock than 11 o'clock.

イギリスの睡眠の専門家は気持ちよく朝起きるためには、９０分のまとまりで起きたい時刻から逆算したほうがいいと述べている。人間は９０分間サイクルで寝ているのだ。９０分以降は、すっきり起きられる状態に一番近くなる。だから、６時に気持ちよく起きるためには、１１時に寝るよりも１２時に寝たほうがいいということだ。

6-1 Artificial Reefs in Mexico （メキシコの人工サンゴ礁）

Off the east coast of Mexico, more than 350 sculptures were installed to create both a unique piece of art and artificial coral reef. The artist hoped to produce a coral reef system that would attract a variety of sea creatures. In recent years, because of the high number of tourists, the nearby natural reefs have suffered a large amount of damage. However, because the sculptures are made of a special concrete ten times harder than normal, they encourage coral growth, creating artwork that is spooky and beautiful, but environmentally friendly at the same time.

メキシコの東岸沖に、３５０個以上の彫刻が置かれ、ひとつのユニークな芸術作品と人工のサンゴ礁の両方を生み出している。その芸術家は様々な海の生き物を魅了するようなサンゴの組織を作りたいと思っていた。ここ数年、かなり多くの観光客のせいで、近くの天然サンゴが大きなダメージを受けている。しかし、その彫刻は通常の１０倍の強度を誇る特別なコンクリートでできているため、サンゴの成長を促し、一方で不気味できれいな作品を形作っている、しかも同時に環境に優しいのだ。

6-2 Bananas （バナナ）

Bananas are one of the world's richest natural sources of vitamins. They contain no fat and have very few calories. By regularly eating bananas in the morning, you not only get a healthy, energetic start to the day, you reduce the risk of heart attack, stroke, and cancer. There are estimated to be over 1000 varieties of banana, which are actually classified as part of the berry family. So bananas are closely related to blueberries, but not strawberries. The strawberry isn't a berry, because it has seeds on the outside. It has its own classification.

バナナは世界で一番ビタミン豊富な天然の供給源のひとつだ。脂質が全くなくカロリーもとても低い。定期的に朝バナナを食べることで、健康的で元気な一日のスタートになるだけではなく、心臓発作や脳卒中、がんの危険性をも低下させる。推計１０００を超える種類のバナナがあり、実はベリーの仲間に分類されている。だからバナナはブルーベリーと密接に関係があるが、イチゴとは関係がない。イチゴはベリーではない、なぜなら種が外側にあるからだ。イチゴはイチゴで分類がある。

6-3 Honey （はちみつ）

If you have a sweet tooth, then you will love honey: a gift of sweetness from Mother Nature. Honey is, of course, made by honey bees. It takes a long time to make honey, and just one teaspoon represents the total lifetime work of 12 bees. Honey has been used as a food for thousands of years, including during ancient times in Egypt. It is used in cooking and also as a natural cure to promote healing of cuts and wounds. Because honey has no use by date, you can keep and use it forever.

もし甘党であれば、はちみつは大好きだろう：母なる自然からの甘い贈り物だ。はちみつは、もちろん、ミツバチによって作られる。はちみつを作るのには長い時間を要し、たったティースプーン一杯のはちみつがハチ１２匹の一生の仕事量の合計に相当する。はちみつは何千年にもわたって食料として使われてきており、古代エジプト時代も含まれる。料理に使われ、そして切り傷やけがの治癒を促進する自然の治療薬としても使われる。はちみつは消費期限がないので、ずっと保存し使うことができるのだ。

6-4 Rainbow Mountains in China （中国の七彩山）

Zhangye Danxia Landform Geological Park in China is home to a mountain range. But these are not your usual green or brown mountains. Over millions of years, a combination of various mineral deposits and red sandstone have layered to create stunning colorful patterns of rainbow colors in the rocks on these mountains. Pictures of these beautiful mountains create images that seem to belong to some kind of exotic alien landscape, but these are certainly on our planet. These colorful mountain patterns have only been observed in China and are quickly becoming a popular tourist attraction.

中国の張掖市（ちょうえきし）丹霞地形（たんかちけい）地層公園は山脈へと続く拠点である。しかし普通の緑や茶色い山ではない。何百万年も、数種類の鉱物の堆積と赤色砂岩の組み合わせが層をなして、この山々の岩にすばらしい虹色の色彩に満ちた模様を生み出してきた。この美しい山々の姿は、ちょっとしたエキゾチックで見知らぬ風景があるような感覚を生み出すが、ちゃんと私たちの惑星にあるのだ。これらのカラフルな山の模様は中国にだけみられ、観光の目玉となりつつある。

6-5 Dolphins （イルカ）

It is common knowledge that dolphins are extremely intelligent animals. They are also known for their agility and playful behavior. But there may be a couple of things you don't know about dolphins. Even though most dolphins live in the sea, they can't drink sea water. They have to get liquid from food they eat, such as fish and squid. They use the blowhole at the top of their heads to breathe, which they must do out of the water. That's why when they sleep, half of their brains stay awake, stopping them from drowning.

イルカは非常に賢い動物であるというのは一般常識である。また俊敏でやんちゃな習性をもつことでも知られている。しかし、イルカについていくつか知らないことがあるかもしれない。イルカは海で生活するにもかかわらず、実は海水を飲めないのだ。口にする食べ物から水分を摂取しなくてはならない、たとえば魚やイカからだ。頭のてっぺんにある噴水孔を使って呼吸をするが、水の外でしなければならない。だから寝るときに、脳の半分は起きたままで、おぼれるのを防いでいるのだ。

List of Vocabulary

Word	Meaning	Level	Word	Meaning	Level
a variety of ~	様々な~	3-4	classification	分類	6-2
actually	実際に	4-3	classify	分類する	6-2
aggressive	攻撃的な	4-5	collect	集める	1-1
agility	軽快さ	6-5	coral reef	サンゴ礁	6-1
alien	地球上のものでない	6-4	cork	コルク	1-2
ancient	古代の	6-3	count back	逆から数える	5-5
Arabic	アラビア語	4-3	cub	小熊	4-5
army	軍隊	4-2	cure	治療	6-3
artificial	人工的	6-1	cycle	周期	5-5
attract	引き寄せる	2-4	defend	守る	4-5
attractive	魅力的	3-5	delicious	美味しい	3-4
biscuit	ビスケット	5-2	deposit	堆積	6-4
bitterly cold	非常に寒い	4-3	desert	砂漠	4-3
blood pressure	血圧	1-5	dirt	汚れ	3-5
bloom	咲く	3-1	distance	距離	1-5
blowhole	噴水孔	6-5	dolphin	イルカ	2-3
body fat	体脂肪	1-5	Down Under	オーストラリア	1-4
bridge	橋	2-4	dozens of ~	数多くの~	1-2
bright	鮮やかな	1-1	dream	夢	3-3
brisk	素早い	1-5	drown	溺れる	6-5
broadcast	放送する	5-4	due to ~	~による	3-2
bulb	球根	3-1	effect	効果	2-5
burst	突発	5-3	electricity	電気	5-3
butterfly	蝶	3-5	encourage	促す	6-1
can't ~ a thing	一つ~も出来ない	4-1	energetic	エネルギッシュ	6-2
cave	洞窟	4-4	enjoy ~ing	~をするのを楽しむ	4-1
celebrate	祝う	3-4	equivalent to ~	~に相当する	1-5

Word	Meaning	Level
estimate	推測する	6-2
exist	存在する	5-4
exotic	エキゾチックな	6-4
expert	専門家	5-5
extremely	極めて	4-3
feel refreshed	気持ち良い	5-5
feel relaxed	落ち着いた気分	1-1
festival	祭り	3-4
fluid	液体	3-2
fortune cookie	おみくじ入りクッキー	5-2
gather	集まる	1-4
giraffe	キリン	1-3
good for ~	～に良い	1-5
gravity	重力	3-2
heal	治す	6-3
heart attack	心臓発作	6-2
hoax	悪ふざけ	5-4
humid	蒸し暑い	1-1
hunt	狩りをする	2-3
in itself	～だけで	4-2
install	設置する	6-1
instead of ~	～の代わりに	3-3
intend	目指す	5-1
invent	発明する	5-2
killer whale	シャチ	2-3
lake	湖	2-2

Word	Meaning	Level
lifetime	一生	1-5
lightning strike	落雷	5-3
liquid	液体	6-5
memory	記憶	2-5
micro~	100万分の1	5-3
mineral	鉱物	6-4
moose	ヘラジカ	4-5
Mother Nature	母なる自然	6-3
mountain range	山脈	6-4
muscle pain	筋肉痛	2-5
nearby	近くに	4-1
neck	首	1-3
North Pole	北極	2-3
nutrient	栄養	5-1
off the coast	沖に	6-1
on average	平均して	1-5
optical illusion	錯視	2-4
orca	シャチ	2-3
participant	参加者	3-4
persimmon	柿	3-3
phrase	ことわざ	4-2
plant (noun)	植物	4-5
plant (verb)	植える	1-1
pray	祈る	5-4
protective	保護的な	4-5
rain forest	熱帯雨林	4-4

Word	Meaning	Level
reason	理由	2-2
reduce	減らす	1-5
refreshing	爽やかな	2-5
repel	はじく	3-5
Roman Empire	ローマ帝国	4-2
room temperature	室温	2-5
salty	しょっぱい	2-2
sandstone	砂岩	6-4
scientist	科学者	2-2
sculpture	彫刻	6-1
seal	アザラシ	2-3
seed	種	1-1
severe	厳しい	4-3
shaped like ~	~の形をしている	2-1
single	独身	2-1
skin	（ボールなどの）外側	1-2
soft toy	ぬいぐるみ	4-5
source	源	6-2
spare a thought for ~	~のことを少し考える	4-3
spine	背骨	3-2
spooky	不気味	6-1
stall	屋台	3-4
state	状態	5-5
strategically	戦略的に	4-2
strike	（雷が）落ちる	5-3
stroke	脳卒中	6-2

Word	Meaning	Level
stunning	極めて美しい	6-4
such as	例えば	3-1
sudden	突然の	5-3
suggest	提案する	5-5
sunflower	ヒマワリ	1-1
sweet tooth	甘党である	6-3
Switzerland	スイス	5-4
taste like ~	~のような味がする	3-3
thirsty	喉が渇いた	4-3
thunderstorm	嵐	5-3
tongue	舌	1-3
transmit	送る	4-1
unique	独特の	2-4
use by date	消費期限	6-3
Venezuela	ベネズエラ	5-3
vitamin	ビタミン	2-5
watermelon	スイカ	2-5
waterproof	防水	3-5
weekend	週末	1-4
wing	羽	3-5
wound	傷	6-3
yarn	糸	1-2

[著者紹介]

Adrian Leis（リース　エイドリアン）
東北学院大学教授。
オーストラリア出身。1997年に来日後、英会話学校、ALT、私立中学校高等学校の教諭（副担任も含む）を経て、現職に至る。2016年に東北大学大学院博士課程を修了し、現在は英語教育、動機づけ、反転学習を中心に研究を行っている。

Simon Cooke（クック　サイモン）
東北工業大学准教授。
イギリス出身。1996年に来日後、ALT、高等学校での勤務を経て、現職に至る。現在は英語教育、動機づけを中心に研究を行っている。

無敵リスニング〈中級〉
Ultimate Listening 〈Intermediate〉

著　者	Adrian Leis・Simon Cooke
発行者	武 村 哲 司
印刷所	萩原印刷株式会社

2017年3月25日　第1版第1刷発行
2019年4月3日　第2版第1刷発行
2024年3月25日　　　第4刷発行

発行所　株式会社 開拓社
〒112-0013 東京都文京区音羽1丁目22番16号
電話 (03)5395-7101 (代表)
振替 00160-8-39587
https://www.kaitakusha.co.jp

© 2019 Adrian Leis and Simon Cooke　　　ISBN978-4-7589-2310-1　C0082

JCOPY 〈出版者著作権管理機構　委託出版物〉
本書の無断複製は著作権法上での例外を除き禁じられています。複製される場合は、そのつど事前に、出版者著作権管理機構（電話 03-5244-5088, FAX 03-5244-5089, e-mail: info@jcopy.or.jp）の許諾を得てください。